Also by MICHAEL LISTA

POETRY
Bloom
The Scarborough

NON-FICTION
Strike Anywhere
The Human Scale

MICHAEL LISTA

BARFLY

and Other Poems

BIBLIOASIS
Windsor, Ontario

FIRST EDITION
10 9 8 7 6 5 4 3 2 1

Library and Archives Canada Cataloguing in Publication
Title: Barfly / Michael Lista.
Names: Lista, Michael, 1983- author.
Identifiers: Canadiana (print) 20230578292 | Canadiana (ebook) 20230578314 |
    ISBN 9781771966115 (softcover) | ISBN 9781771966122 (EPUB)
Classification: LCC PS8623.I85 B37 2024 | DDC C811/.6—dc23

Edited and designed by Vanessa Stauffer
Copyedited by John Sweet
Cover/interior illustration: Evgeny Turaev/Shutterstock

 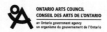 

Published with the generous assistance of the Canada Council for the Arts, which last year invested $153 million to bring the arts to Canadians throughout the country, and the financial support of the Government of Canada. Biblioasis also acknowledges the support of the Ontario Arts Council (OAC), an agency of the Government of Ontario, which last year funded 1,709 individual artists and 1,078 organizations in 204 communities across Ontario, for a total of $52.1 million, and the contribution of the Government of Ontario through the Ontario Book Publishing Tax Credit and Ontario Creates.

PRINTED AND BOUND IN CANADA

for Genevieve, who changed my mind

Contents

Forgive Me, Leonard · 11

Auld Lang Syne · 15
My Body Is a Temple · 18
Kids · 19
Putin · 21
Able Archer · 22
Based on a Story by Michael Lista · 26
Dealing with Fans · 27
The Bill · 29
America · 31
Cats · 32
On the Disappearance of Roughly Eleven Billion
    Crabs and the Cessation of Alaska's Fishery · 34
Traitorous Former Editors & Cultural Apparatchiks · 36
What It's Like to Write a Book · 37
Booze · 38
Towards a Theory of Contemporary Poetry · 39
Bar Fights · 41
Battle Raps · 42
Nose Beers · 44
War · 46
Hamlet, Hamlet · 47
Job, 23, in Hollywood · 49
The Zoo · 51
Draughts · 52
Sports · 53
Beethoven's Ninth Symphony, 3/5 Stars · 54
Freedom Convoy · 56

Mum · 57

Snow · 58

Alea Iacta Est · 59

The Yips · 61

Merkins · 62

Carmine · 65

I Have a Gun in My Mouth · 66

I Want to Go to Mount Baldy · 67

What If God Was One of Us? · 69

Jeff · 70

Fuck You · 71

Going to the Moon · 72

Apollo 11 · 73

Lebensraum · 74

Identity Theft · 76

My Love · 78

Clouds · 79

Reasons to Live · 80

The Bar in Hell · 82

Sartre? · 84

Dusk · 85

Earth · 86

One Last Shot of Jameson · 87

Barfly · 88

Hungover · 97

Acknowledgements · 99

"Hamlet"
—HAMLET

Forgive Me, Leonard

I knew literature had lost the battle
Once bookstores started selling scented candles

And hanging banners—once he'd died—of Leonard Cohen
Above baskets of shawls from Patagonia.

The guy wrote: "Give me crack and anal sex,"
But the market wanted tea-and-orange-scented Durex,

And his other famous crack, the one in everything—
Though opinions, they say, are like assholes:

That's how the light gets in.

Auld Lang Syne

There used to be too many things anyway—
Plans and people and places to go.

If you weren't careful, you could waste
A whole day with someone else.

The movies stretched fifty feet high,
Went on forever, and smelled like popcorn

And kissing. My favourite bar
Didn't even get to drink itself to death.

It died of thirst
And loneliness, and didn't even wait

For me to go first.
Before it was zilch

The pay was a pittance.
Good riddance

To baseball, which was even more boring in person
Because everyone was smaller in real life, whatever

That was, and you had to walk so far and wait so long for a beer.
Let's be clear:

Someone could call you out of nowhere
And say, "I miss you"

And then you'd have to cook them pasta,
Listen to Duke Ellington, and dance

Until one of you said *basta*.
Worst was that it felt like it was going somewhere,

All of it, proceeding to a point,
Arranging like a spider with its web,

But when it went,
The long nights and handshakes and work,

It proved itself figment
And fragment,

A thin hypothesis
In the process of disproof, then

Poof.
Now you can't even vanish

In plain sight. You disappear
Into the year.

Whoever loves you can't even volunteer
To be there.

Shopping lives on
Like lichen,

And won't die. I'd kill for a high-five,
Or a fair fight.

You can't even get your ass kicked anymore.
I wish I could say, "What survives of us is love,"

But love was first to go.
Bread stayed,

And booze, thank god,
And you.

It still rains.
And I can still complain

That the sky is sometimes somehow blue,
Like some smug proof.

You can still shut the lights off,
And even turn them on if you want to.

My Body Is a Temple

My body is a temple,
The kind you hack into with a machete,

Reclaimed by jungle centuries ago,
Overrun with jaguars and banyans,

The shaman long since slaughtered, the god absconded,
A ruin now, a whole religion lost,

Its parish just the sun and rain and dark,
The elements its book of common prayer,

Though still a fine place for a pretty tourist
And her short Australian boyfriend, on a lark,

To search for something dumb, like truth or beauty,
And as one of my anacondas encloses, he'll say:

God, I'm so glad we came here baby.

Kids

Why does everyone want kids?
My friend's kid, whose identity I'm protecting,

Has this problem right now
Of sticking their finger

Up their own asshole,
And then

Smelling
It

And everyone
In their class has worms.

Everyone who wanted to fuck me once
Left me because I wouldn't give her kids.

I can be a Canadian poet about it
And yammer on about science,

Though even Newton
Knew when

To shut up.
Hot take: no one should be born.

Having kids is actually kind of mean.
Who are you to say I have to live?

You didn't like the people you already had
So let the old wheel spin and begat—

You aren't a parent;
You're a gambler with a diaper bill.

They do it for the pictures,
Holding a smiling potato

Who will get bad grades and go bankrupt
Or do well and be low-key corrupt.

Parents are theatre kids who didn't learn
An audience is something that you earn.

Don't procreate. Be a writer: get a page
Which, although blank, at least will never age,

Avoiding that whole superseding void,
The immensity of having to grow old,

For what, a Polaroid—
So you could smile and hold a baby

In the 1980s?

Putin

The French press
God bless them

Calls Putin
"Poutine."

He's insane,
Wants Ukraine,

And while everyone has covid,
I lie in bed reading Ovid,

Watching CNN where Biden says
That if it's just a mild invasion

It's cool. The world has Omicron
And Poutine can have Omukraine

But then he'll have to eat the porcupine.

Able Archer

Not if but when it ends, the world will end
By accident, with one guy pressing Send,

Not with a whimper, but with a bang—
Eliot knew dick about the bomb.

Four-piece suits and verse plays—he's your man.
The fucking guy became an Anglican.

I Anglican't
Even.

So seat me at the tiki bar with a Mai Tai
On Bikini Atoll, and say it's not high time

To let the dice roll.
Say it's November 1983

Two months after September 1, 1983,
When I was born, and Korean Air

Flight 007—lol—
Was shaken, not stirred, from the Soviet skies

Because they thought the passengers were spies.
When Reagan branded them the Evil Empire

He had such great hair
When talking to the press and said: *beware*

Of Star Wars—lol—which the Reds thought was unfair
Because it could blow their missiles from the air

Such that we couldn't kill each other equally
And every other living thing, fair and square.

Then nato conducted a routine—lol—
War game about the end of the world

Called Able Archer,
With farm boys from Iowa on the phone

Saying both *this is not a drill, I swear it,*
And also—so the Reds could hear it—

Exercise Exercise Exercise
So those damn dirty Russkies surmised

The mushroom clouds would come as a surprise
In the form of an exercise.

The world was about to end, Old Possum,
And nobody knew it was happening.

nato flew KC-130s to the Russian border
Trying to hear what they would say

Before veering away.
The Stalinists had spies in Washington,

Counting how many lights were on
In the Pentagon.

Andropov clutched his nuclear football
From his hospital bed, in kidney failure,

And put his whole arsenal on alert,
Sending mobile ss-20s into forests,

Submarines under the Arctic ice,
Finally putting a cost to every price,

Ever the Marxist.
This made the Cuban Missile Crisis

Look like a mild case of gastritis.
Then one Russian, farting in his chair,

Saw a missile coming through the air
And then another, from America,

And almost shit himself, having a BM
As five more ICBMS—

All Minutemen—
Made us all minute-by-minute men.

What saved the world was that this Russian knew
If America wanted to fuck you, she would fuck you

Not piece by piece, one nuke at a time,
But all at once, and she'd make it rhyme.

The missiles ended up, thank Parnassus,
Just being the sun reflecting off the asses

Of a couple
Of clouds.

So he stood Russia down,
And the world didn't end,

Except for Andropov, whose kidneys failed,
And Reagan, whose mind was mailed

Somewhere without a return to sender,
So I could grow up to be so tender.

Based on a Story by Michael Lista

I have a TV show now
Though no one to watch it with.

I haven't seen it
But

Apparently it's like me
With more people in it.

I can still count to five:
Me, us, everyone else—

Anyways, what is this, Math?
I'm too rich to count anything but money.

In the aggregate, as a principle, life
Was

—Fine? I'd peg it at
Three

Out of five.
Like me, it was a natural

C student, so round
Down

And cling
To whoever's still around.

Dealing with Fans

Everyone hates my writing
Except Ironman

Who made it rain during a drought
Of doubt.

I marvel that the marvel of it is
That I was always a DC kid

And as the two readers of my poems know
(Sorry to out you, Jason

And Carmine)
I only ever wanted to be Superman,

Wearing a suit as thin
As my skin,

Bounding from kitten
To kitten

In need of saving,
Pounding

My X-ray vision
Into whoever can make a decision:

I AM SUPERMAN
AND I AM SO BROKEN

I'D TRADE ANY MIND
FOR MINE

It's like what Sloan said
(But stood on its head):

What sucks isn't the fans
But their band.

The Bill

John Thompson, John Thompson, John Thompson—we
Get it: you've read

A ghazal.
Even having had a couple,

And even having had been an occasional couple,
I still leave a little to guzzle

When the bill comes,
Just in case I realize I'm talking about the thing

I was just talking about.
White, folded

Right down the middle,
You look at it and go:

This is where cops get their haircuts.
I think it'll be a trifle

But is almost always something worth messing with
The way any measurement is.

I've got it, because listen, getting away
With getting away with pretty much everything

Since, well,
When did we start keeping count,

Is like jumping onto a running horse,
Which I've never done,

But would
And would look so cool if you could.

In the end
It's an end, fine

And what are a couple of drinks,
And whatever we once were, between friends?

It'll be on me and I'll walk home, then
Turn onto my street and want to say to anyone:

The scary thing about literature
Is that it's dangerously close

To talking to yourself.
Then blow the pistol smoke,

Pew, from my fingers,
Do the holster thing in my coat pockets, and remember

I only write poems
—And trust me, I try not to—

When my heart is really broken
Which ended up being most of the time.

America

It's a banana republic
Wearing Banana Republic

Manufactured in a banana republic
And remaindered to a Banana Republic

Outlet
Store,

Like tortoises
But turtlenecks

All the way down.

Cats

Sometimes I look at my elderly cats
And think:

Fuck you, sunshine.
I'm going to have to live to watch you die.

It will be cold out, warm inside, and sunny.
Then you'll cough weird and look at me funny.

You were really fucking with my sex game, by the way—
Women trust a man who has a dog,

Not two old broken tabbies,
Pouncing and plunging like quotation marks

When dad's just trying to get some ass.
First-round draft picks have less sass:

Here comes the land shark, like a trucker
Plunking his semi in front of Parliament,

With a look in his eye like I'm his mark,
And I am.

I am,
Little man.

So what
If I love you, asshole.

Don't you realize the day will come
When I will have to, hurriedly, wherever I can,

Pump the darkness into your veins,
Walk out of the vet's, try not to go insane,

Recite my postal code, my date of birth,
My name, and wonder where you went,

Though everything we love is like money or pills—
You only get them to get rid of them.

On the Disappearance of Roughly Eleven Billion Crabs and the Cessation of Alaska's Fishery

Bro—
Where did all the motherfucking crabs go?

And how in the name of You Know Who
Are they going to film *Deadliest Catch*

Now that that deadliest catch
Up and collapsed?

Legally, they can only catch males
And my boys said: screw this—I'm outie, peace,

You jerks will have to just eat lobster now.
But bro, seriously though:

Where did all the motherfucking crabs go?
Maybe they're chilling on a UFO,

Getting gobbled up by aliens,
Or taking the year off to read Jordan Peterson,

To really study him, as a person,
And, as he suggests on page one hundred and who-gives-a-shit,

To exercise,
Getting exercised about illegal aliens,

Founding creepy men's clubs,
Measuring each other's sad half chubs,

Yelling over one another about Gender Theory
And the actually fascinating history behind why keyboards spell
   QWERTY,

And just high-fiving, seriously bro-ing out
On the Bering Sea floor, running out

Of jokes in the Mariana Trench,
Dreaming of sunshine, getting good at bench,

Skipping a season like a leg day—
Though it might be nice, one thinks, to hazard a lady.

Traitorous Former Editors & Cultural Apparatchiks

The problem with calling someone a monster
Is that they start to wonder

Is that who you want me to be?
Being good, that someone will go

Where you send them,
With a hunger, with a sentence,

That only expires
Once one of you is senescent,

Into the dark, lower than where you dream,
To grow and grow and grow and grow and grow.

What It's Like to Write a Book

You know you're onto something
Once your manuscript is just fat enough

To roll up
And swat the fly

You've finally
Come to like.

Booze

They say it's bad for you
But if that was true

How come it makes you feel so good?
And how come

Unlike everyone else
It won't leave you?

My favourite is a snort at four a.m.
When I wake in absolute terror

And know that pretty much every woman
Who once liked me

Is being woken in absolute terror
By a baby who looks nothing like me.

Towards a Theory of Contemporary Poetry

It is difficult to get a man to understand something when his salary depends on his not understanding it.
—UPTON SINCLAIR

If you're going to forget how to talk,
Don't do it like that laurelled cock

Whose poems stopped making sense to anybody
Without even making them funny.

His best work recently was on Facebook,
Where all the angry aunts and uncles lurk,

When he said he thought of punching me in the throat
Because of an essay that I wrote.

I had to hand it, like a prize, to the man—
Finally: a line that one could scan.

He'd insinuated that he'd break my neck
But was just a feckless teacher's pet,

An obtuse, obscure bro on sabbatical
Since he decided to be radical.

Here's a theory of Canadian poetry:
It's chickenshit, just obtuse imagery,

Prestigious, albeit a little late,
Egregious, lily-white Latinate,

Belated Anglo-Saxon set on farms,
Swanning consonants of false alarms,

Anne Carson, Anne Carson, and uh oh right:
Anne Carson,

Bad self-help, the infliction of harm
Dressed up as wellness but devoid of charm,

The propping up of local famous kings
Who pay you nothing to say nothing,

Ninety-seven percent open letters
And three percent drunk paper tigers,

Prescription drugs and hollow threats of violence,
Congratulatory tweets, thugs and silence,

Going on and on about CBC,
CBD, CBT,

Anything but whiskey, THC,
Or me,

Has-beens and never-weres who want prizes, Nikes,
And to devour psyches,

And I want to tell them: you can, you could,
If only you'd pivot to Hollywood.

Bar Fights

Buddy wants to distract me from my gin,
And the poem I was writing, with a grin,

Acting tougher than he's ever been,
And staring, with a plan, into my chin.

Personally, I'd prefer to dance
With someone pretty, who I'd meet by chance

En route to the jukebox, sharing a glance
Then settling down for the vast expanse

Of a one-night stand.
On the other hand,

I could lend him my head to break his hand,
And listen as his knuckles turn to sand,

Since men are manufactured for their breaking:
Born on sale, just there for the taking.

Battle Raps

Have you seen *Amy?*
The documentary about Amy Winehouse?

I watched it in Banff the night Amy,
Another Amy, the love of my life,

Was getting married to somebody else,
And I was sleeping with somebody else's

Wife
And thought it was—get this—

Love. Like:
What a life.

Right at the end of, before,
Well, you know,

She drinks herself to death,
She calls her bodyguard

And is like:
I've got all these battle raps pouring out of me

And
Looking back at her own life,

Baffled, unloved, pretty, and pretty lit,
Says to the guy paid to protect her: *I could sing, man*

And then this huge Jamaican guy, he goes:
I know, I know, as if he was innocent

As if her most salient fact
Was something the muscle might get wrong

Then she poured
One more

And left like a song.

Nose Beers

I'm only screwing chicks from Parkdale now.
They're bad, show up two at a time, and *how*,

Live down the street, and get kicked onto it
By that dick bartender who's had enough of their shit.

No one in Toronto has a sense of humour
Except these birds, who can make you a rumour,

Fuck you properly,
Then steal your property,

And talk the sort of shit about you
That, even at your own expense, you're kind of into.

They're better good trouble than John Lewis,
With eyes as chestnut as the Rhino's bar,

Calling themselves—*themselves*—"these little bitches"
And saying shit like: "snitches get stitches"

And when their moms ask: "Aren't you afraid of Parkdale?"
Say: "I'm what to be afraid of in Parkdale."

And they're hot.
And hey I'm not

Condoning them—getting banned from every bar
On Queen Street from Jameson to Ossington,

Inviting you back to theirs,
Jameson in their hair,

Where they'll call everybody they know
Scouring for blow,

Dancing down Queen with a bottle, giving every asshole a cheers,
Cooing: "Yo—who's got the nose beers?"

I bed the one who just got out of jail
(For telling a cop to go fuck himself, for the hell

Of it all),
Because she keeps insisting that I'm tall.

They had her on a twelve-hour hold—
As long as she held me from getting old.

War

The creative writing teachers were wrong.
Don't find your voice—

Lose it,
Then fight like hell for having lost it.

Stay frosty,
Your voice a little froggy,

Like an insurgent with a fresh AK
And nothing original to say.

Hamlet, Hamlet

Whenever someone complains
Now I just look at them and say:

Hamlet.

Oh your wife left you?
Hamlet.

You have testicular cancer?
Hamlet.

I published a mixed review of your sophomore effort eleven years ago?
Hamlet.

The world collapsed around you,
Took all your little chicks

And their hen?
Hamlet.

You were there
When the last elephant

Was murdered for its tusk,
Watched its luxurious eyelashes

Close upon
Its dark wet fulminating eye,

So some Dogecoin investor in Zhejiang
Could carve an ivory elephant for his fiancée,

As a wedding present,
And you weren't just present,

But pulled the trigger, and were not hesitant
To cut its tail off for Instagram?

—actually that's more Macbeth.

Job, 23, in Hollywood

When I haven't been laid in a while, I miss God, and think:
   We should break into His house.
Lying in bed unfucked, I wonder: Where does He live?
   I'll bet myself a thousand bucks it isn't church, duh.
Find the finest villa
   On the highest of the Hollywood hills,
Kick in the door,
   Waving the four-four
Like Biggie,
   Fight through His hundred bodyguards,
Pedophiles all, and their hundred hard-ons,
   Slapping their hairless dicks away
Like heresies
   To find God's satin smoking jacket laid on His revolving circular bed
Modelled after Hugh Hefner's,
   Covered in the blood
Of everyone He doesn't love
   And be like:
What is the Almighty going to do, call the cops?
   It's a victimless crime. He's God. I was just curious
And He isn't even home.

I still look for him, though,
   East into Silverlake
And He's not there.
   I drive west to the Chateau Marmont,
Find nothing but Belushi's ghost.
   When He sets up a tech company in San Francisco
I can't reach Him, even by sending Him money on Venmo.
   His mind bends south towards Mexico
With this coyote I know
   Who has really good blow,

And a dozen suitcases full of dough.
    I hope He's like Alexa or Siri,
Barely pretending not to hear me,
    When He's tested me, and I've wanted Him
To text me,
    Hearing me weep at a greeting card in a Florida Publix,
The one about the footsteps,
    Where God hides your tracks
By giving you a piggyback
    Which right now doesn't sound so bad.

But God's more aloof than a deadbeat dad,
    Having fucked off
Since the Bronze Age to—I don't know,
    Bowl, or play golf,
Surveille and speculate
    In the one corner of the Levant
Where there isn't
    Even
Any oil.
    But I can just feel, wherever he is, He hates me—
Someone I love
    Will leave me,
An editor will tell me I'm toxic
    For having published exactly what he wanted,
Someone I slept with once will write in *Esquire*
    That I'm a monster for not having married her,
And I'm terrified again in front of God.
    Even translating this now, I'm afraid before You
Especially since I can't read Hebrew.
    Wherever God is, He can still make me blush
Like I'm some dark-haired blue-eyed thing
    In Jersey on a date with Bruce Springsteen
Riding the Ferris wheel as long as he needs
    Until He's ready to sing.

The Zoo

I can't think when I'm in love,
But out of it, there's nothing to think of.

Love fits me as a hand assumes a glove,
Or how the air accommodates a dove,

Goes white with it, then flutters back to blue.
Everything makes me think of you,

How once there was just one, then there were two,
My mind as full and captive as a zoo

With you and you and you and you and you.

Draughts

Draughts
Like drafts

Get better
The more you keep working on them.

Though working on them
Alas

Is just as likely to make you bitter
As better.

Sports

The Olympics is just power eating,
You know, where one kid competes to see if he can eat more hot
   dogs than everyone else,

For kids too rich or thin or shy or vain
To admit that they're in pain.

Beethoven's Ninth Symphony, 3/5 Stars

So
Yo

The horseshit thing
About Beethoven's Ninth Symphony

Is that
All of a sudden,

Almost at the end,
There's suddenly

German
In it.

Some lederhosen-
Wearing

Kraut
Has the nuts

To shout
About—what:

Goethe
Or Hitler, joy,

Exterminating
The Jews,

Tiny
Moustaches

Techno,
Tiësto,

Whatever those
Guys were into.

There's no accounting for taste
Though I thought the whole point, the stakes,

All those grass-mowed graves on Omaha
And Juno Beach,

Was that human music doesn't belong
To anyone.

How jejune of me.

Freedom Convoy

Everyone I've loved is out of my league.
Like Ottawa police chief Sloly,

I let my betters get the best of me,
Lying there like a city under siege,

Her bouncy castles congesting my infrastructure,
Her semis seizing my Ambassador—

Even when she's wrong, I've wanted her.

Mum

I loved having had been your son
But that's a David Foster Wallace reference

So, finger across my throat as a sad white writer dude in 2021
—*Kckkk*—with some hesitance

I worry I very well may be done.

Snow

It makes me feel like someone's up above.
It falls like drunks down a fire escape.

It's like love—
Pretty as hell and hard to navigate.

Alea Iacta Est

Alea Iacta Est,
The die is cast,

So what, I'm supposed to just kiss
Julius Caesar's ass

Because he crossed the Rubicon
What—once?

I've marched my moonlit legion
Across a thousand streams, into regions

Caesar would have drowned in like a lake—
I sank Margaret Atwood for Christ's sake.

He won the Battle of Alesia
But didn't live to hear the YouTube hit "Aicha,"

He defeated Vercingetorix
So we could watch the reboot of *The Matrix.*

The poor old man has made his bed
So should be allowed to die in it.

The lie of it
Is that

Jesus was waiting nearby in the wings
With, well, that whole Christianity thing.

Anyways, he was more into baptisms
Than sending whole armies across rivers,

More a bath guy
Than a horse and blood and guts and math guy.

If Caesar wanted to see Rome, Jesus,
He could have waited for Ryanair like the rest of us.

But from my limited vantage point
Living liminal

At this late date
I'm no limnologist

Ergo
I don't know

Who to hate
When everything happened so long ago.

The Yips

Yup
I've got the yips

Yips
To publish

Yips
To kiss

Yips
To even exist.

If Simone Biles
Could unpile

So can this.

Merkins

It's getting so bad
My dad's girlfriend is trying to set me up,

Not for failure but—just get this—for love.
She can summon affection, and say: leave

With this auburn-haired brilliant friend of mine
For anywhere, packing just your own minds.

She sounds kind, insufferable, and mindful,
And if it's not made up, my mind is full,

And anyways where is there anywhere
To ever be with anyone anymore?

Where is there to go
With someone you don't know,

After all of us have had to hone
How to be so exquisitely alone?

Even Rome is all Virgil and virgins,
Cheap dresses and designer lingerie

Which you won't see until your wedding day,
Exchange students growing their own merkins,

While mirthless
You creep the Pantheon's waxed oculus.

She'll ask me something dumb, piercing, and true,
Like: So you were a poet once, weren't you?

She'll sound like a sweetheart,
But then I'll snap, and say if I were Kmart

I wouldn't stock some droopy flower
Like Rupi Kaur—

If I wanted to make money and have fun
I wouldn't sell *milk and honey.* I'd sell guns.

My date's more
Eat, Pray, Love

And to date I'm more
Drink, Swear, Fuck.

I don't want to heal—
Like Redman, I want to rob and steal.

Boring women talk about therapists,
Boring men talk about Republicans,

And there it is:
Nobody can shut up about their dreams.

To have a dream
Is to have a dram

Of some old sacred slippery secret thing
You have to hold on to

Against everything, with all it demands,
A fabric fabricated out of sand

That you have to dare to try to hand to
The hand of someone that you almost knew.

And then one must choose:
Learn how to keep a fist and follow through

Or let it again as always just fall through.

I text the ex I don't deserve to miss
And we reminisce

About how weird it was that it was true
That neither of us knew

Why we broke up
So hung up, we hung up.

Carmine

The person I've always wanted to be
Said he lives vicariously though me—

Now what am I supposed to do,
Live?

I Have a Gun in My Mouth

I have a gun in my mouth
Kidding—what is this, America?

I can't get a gun. I'm not Kyle Rittenhouse.
But in my house

You can lay all of history on your tongue
And pray it's taken out by anyone.

I Want to Go to Mount Baldy

I want to go to Mount Baldy,
Take my vow of silence,

Look around for a hot second
Then whisper to the baldest monk around:

Bro
I'm afraid that I'm balding

And each of my once-held thoughts
Feels like it's falling from me like a hair.

Then he'd Kung-Fu chop me,
Pow, right in my receding hairline

And go: Bro
We all know.

Leonard Cohen said they drank whiskey together
As often as Achilles fought Hector

And my own tiny monk
Would go:

Listen Baldy—can I call you Baldy?—
At least the spectre

Of Phil Spector
Isn't around to put a gun to your head

To ruin
Another one of your records

Because fuck his wall of sound
That bald fuck.

What If God Was One of Us

What if God was one of us?
I'd bet He'd vape

And be vague
And stay up too late

And go on and on about Karl Ove Knausgaard
And have half as many Twitter followers

As his own parody account, @God.
And we'd all roll our eyes

And he'd nod
And try to hide that he wasn't surprised.

Jeff

Jeff—
You saw my dick and balls in the Bahamas

When you knocked on my door needing my vape
And I was T-nakes.

I'm sorry
That you've now beheld my glory.

Let's get sauced
And wander the world's hotels getting lost.

If my sister wasn't your baby mama
I'd still call you my brother-in-law.

I want people to look at us with awe
And then be like *aww* ...

I'd say *I love you*
But you wouldn't want me to,

Because you have everything on the planet in your truck
Except a single solitary fuck.

Fuck You

Shall
I call

This
Book

Fuck You
& other poems

?
?

No one's done it yet.
It will be like landing on the moon

And giving Earth the finger
Even as you miss it, gasping in your spacesuit,

Radioing Armstrong like *ckshhh*:
"One petty step for all mankind,"

Beholding Heaven
But wanting to go home.

Going to the Moon

It looks like a beach
But without an ocean

And no bar
Plus it's so far

And there's no view
Of the moon.

Yet I've come all this way
So *ckshhh:*

"Uh, ahem,
For all mankind:

Can we read someone other than
Anne Carson?"

Apollo II

Dudes are so dumb.
The moon isn't for going to—

It's for looking at,
When you're alone with your cat,

Trying to prolong
The hair of the dog

With something earthy and bitter.
It's like Twitter:

Fine, tweet, but don't buy the whole fucking thing
Like some crazed South African clown.

The moon will never be a town;
Just let it stumble through heaven and frown.

Lebensraum

I wrote all these poems
In my living room,

Standing up
For nothing for a change

And for a break, to lighten it up,
I'd listen to podcasts about Hitler

Who was always going on
About living room,

Living room,
Living room,

Like a mad interior
Decorator.

So, standing in my living room,
Avoiding Zoom,

Am I now
Yo

Literally
—Hitler?

Maybe
I should poll Twitter.

Nein.
If I were a Fräulein

I wouldn't furrow
A frown line

Worrying any further
Mein Führer.

Identity Theft

No one wants to steal my identity
Because: do it—then you'll have to be me,

Making stupid jokes about going mad,
Since they were the only jokes you had,

Dumb shit like: if you get cancelled for anything,
They send you to this psychiatric ward,

A very special psychiatric ward
Called, wait for it, the Twitter Wing.

Boom: genius.
I pretty much *am*

Netflix.
Jealous?

I'm also, by the way, an empty costume
Without you,

And I
Can't even start to say how much I miss you,

How much and who I'd kill
To get the thrill

To—and this is an issue—
Kiss you,

And okay fine you can drive my car
But it can only take us so far,

The seat heaters on, with nowhere to go,
And my arm around you.

My Love

It was close there for a hot sec—
Sure, we had a lot of yummy sex,

To your mind not enough,
Though let's not get into all that stuff,

And what were we supposed to do: Marry?
You're not Meghan Markle. I'm no Harry.

We're in love, but we're still millennials.
What's wrong with our hearts is congenital.

We don't possess the romance, the patience
Of our hidebound, sturdy grandparents,

And the innovation of their kids, our folks,
Is they could turn their vows into our jokes.

Clouds

Shall I eat
Or shall I kill myself?

I'm hungry
For something

But who knows.
The clouds go on their business being clouds—

Look one way, and they're clouds
Then another second they're gone.

Clouds
Are

The punctuation
Of the sky

—mint that, it's a bumper sticker.

Reasons to Live

Fine—fuck you—I'll stay and love this life,
Though life's the mad one brandishing the knife,
Cutting down its lovely creatures,
Disfiguring the very features
It bestowed, and we all came to like.

Yeah, we get it, Earth, you gaveth all
But also, dude, so too you taketh all,
Like everybody's beauty
Which was the whole reason to get booty,
Back in the days when we still screwed at all.

Though why admit that something's beautiful
When it will just make fun of you, or fall
And break its pretty neck
Which you'd kissed, tried to protect,
And studied how it swallowed Adderall.

Every atom of me wants to hate you,
This stranded rock that gets to create you,
And since I won't quit it,
I should be allowed to hit it
With curses, and my twisted sense of virtue.

Reasons to live.
One: there is nothing else.
Two: everyone can only be themselves.
Three: if I won't do it
Someone else will screw it
Up, each of us locked in our separate cells,

Prisoners to knowing that we know,
Chilly on heaven, and lukewarm on hell.

The Bar in Hell

It doesn't ever close.
You'd need a firehose
To clean the locals out,
And even then they'd just go on burning,

Reminiscing,
Kissing
The lip of their gin,
Still full of who they almost could have been.

We know, we know, you think it isn't fair
To still be homesick for that vanished world
And the big man who banished you from it
But every god is Saturn, and eats his sons,

Plus there's a new boss now, the bro with horns,
And though the patrons say *the devil may care,*
They really mean he doesn't, and never will,
About anything but the bill, which you pay for with your soul.

But who ever needed a soul anyway? They're for throwing away.
That's the great thing about Hell—
Everyone can finally be themselves,
A girl who doesn't love you on your arm,

A forbidden song in your heart,
A minor affair in a minor key.
And the bar in Hell is never empty—
It's packed. I'm talking wall-to-wall whole snacks,

And though there isn't room for everyone,
Everyone belongs. Dude: you can Tinder
Until your swiping finger is tender
And still not fall in love again, thank God.

Just pick a stranger, and do the human dance,
Wagering your lost soul on your last romance—
It's what landed everybody here,
And there's no one to behave for anymore.

Sartre?

It was one of those pretentious French pricks
Who said that Hell was other people. No one picks

Who loves them,
But once you leave them,

Hell is a bar after last call, empty—
Just me, my Everest of empties,

And all my summited, fading memories
Of thee.

Dusk

The sun is setting on Parkdale,
And everyone is procuring what will prevail

Until tomorrow—
Beer for me,

Via Uber Eats

And for my neighbours in the abandoned building across the
    street
Fentanyl? I guess? Whatever's coming off the Vice desk,

Whatever makes them stumble around in our shared dusk
With their shirts off

While I have a closet full of them
And they have no one to take care of them,

Anything for everyone to fight the sorrow
Of tomorrow,

And tomorrow and tomorrow.
It lengthens, that asshole Shakespeare wrote,

As it grows. It—what the fuck is *it?*
Whatever. He never lived in Parkdale.

Though I wonder what my Nonno would do:
Go, he'd say, blindly with just yourself, go.

Earth

I, speaking for myself, always liked it.
It was always something fun to fight with,

Always someone to go out at night with,
Driving to the mall and getting stoned.

But there was that whole problem with hearts—
They still keep breaking down, and it still hurts.

There's nothing left to do with them. What's worse
Is they aren't going anywhere, and fast.

And someone's heart out there will be the last.

One Last Shot of Jameson

I'm running out of ways to break my heart
While the world, that cheater, had a head start.

Barfly

It calls to me, my final vocation,
To fall out of time, my family on vacation,

From the wooden joist, the bar, the crossbeam,
From which I would hoist—don't be cross—me,

Then drop
Then stop.

It hangs there calling while I watch TV,
And gains a following when it's just me,

Enters my mind like a line of poetry,
Inters what's kind, and calls me a pussy

For delaying our engagement, that I am not
Obeying our arrangement to tie the knot,

Not like a couplet
But like a couple,

And cripple the creeping suspicion
That I'm too simple a being for the mission

At hand—to take life's hand
In my fake brief hand

And say: I do.
Hey: I do.

Dying first among your friends isn't atrocious—
It's precocious

Innovative
Even

And if the kids don't think it's cool
Fuck them—make them study it in school.

A line of poetry
Should be a battery,

A volley of arrows at a barricade
So we can fight in the shade

And be darkly in what we have made,
Our diaphanous parade,

As dire
As diarrhea.

A line of poetry
Should be a party,

Short
Enough to snort

Between archers'
Departures.

Fuck wellness—
Leave that for the rich kids in the West,

Whose parents bought them Pelotons
And go on and on about Lululemon.

Being healthy is for narcissists—
Bring me poetry and narcotics,

Anything true you can deliver
On the reflective side of a liver.

What do I worry about?
What do I worry about—

Drinking, law, and suicide,
Thinking: huh, that's you and I,

Everything we always knew inside,
Anything but what we dared decide.

I'm wasted, wrong, and not all right,
I've waited around too long in the light.

If someone, again, wants to cancel me
I'll lend a hand, spare the hassle: hey:

I'll hand myself the rope,
Even tag you when I tweet about letting 'er rip.

You need a huge vocabulary to scare me,
And you haven't read enough to be as scary

As
Me

Although
I'm so

Alone that if they write my obit
They'll bemoan that I couldn't even get covid.

Killing yourself is more work than you'd think.
It's a logistical nightmare, people to thank,

Contracts to sign, cases of booze to drink,
Hitmen to hire, having to convince

Unconvincing shrinks
That what stinks

Is that whole *to be or not to be*
Because as for T.S. Eliot, it doesn't speak to me.

I don't want to be Hamlet
Because I, too, don't like *Hamlet,*

Hamlet,
Hamlet—

Bruh
I'm not Kenneth Branagh

And if you no longer love the masterpieces
You can't long linger before paying the price.

The rope is rough and cold.
I've had enough and I am old

Though if I have to get to the point
Then I have to get to the point

So in essence
I'm afraid of making sense.

I'd rather make money
And be funny,

Anything but frank.
Staring at the bar, I give thanks—

It's like jazz
Without all the pizzazz,

A bass line, omnivorous, terrible,
From which my timorous treble

Could tremblingly tumble,
Shrinking my temple

To a thimble.
The trick is not thinking about people,

The women who once loved me, in sundresses,
The way someone looks when she undresses,

The surmise
In her eyes,

The surprise
At the first sign of sunrise,

Or your best friend's voice
Ordering off, bereft, your vice,

A cold drink
After a cold dip and a think in the cold lake,

On the porch after rain, long-off lightning
Too far away for thunder, logged off and listening

To something frightening,
Like music, or laughter, or anything,

The sped-up galaxies of fireflies
Accelerated in your sister's eyes,

The sinking feeling
About thinking, feeling

That poems are just feats of engineering
For people who enjoy their injured feelings

And that real life, the good stuff, doesn't rhyme
Since living's good enough, and hasn't time.

I shall affix myself to that high standard,
My tall dominatrix with her hand out,

Calling me to the bar.
The falling won't be far

However fathomless the failing
So don't be blue

Because if you really want me to,
I cross my heart, promise, and hope to die,

To hope, to try
To want to care to haunt whoever's there

When the soldiers call to my ghost: Who's there?

Hungover

Who's there?
Me, what's left of my hair

And more than my fair share,
The scare

I put in the people who care,
That I would dare

Be so unfair.
My chair

Glazed in moonlight that swims the air
Where I can work, where I can bear

To keep my vigil of the world, to stare
At all its brokenness, its ready snare,

And dare it do what it would dare.
Blow winds. Blow until your cheeks crack. I'm here,

Still here, cracking a beer
And toasting ourselves hopeful with a cheers.

Acknowledgments

"The Bar in Hell" originally appeared in *The Walrus*. My thanks to Carmine Starnino for publishing it, and for his friendship.

Thanks to the couplet king, Jason Guriel, il miglior fabbro, who made an early draft of these ditties better.

To the brilliant team at Biblioasis—Emily; my editor, Vanessa; and Dan—for their faith in this book. It was a joy to make it together.

And as always, to my family and friends.

MICHAEL LISTA is a journalist, essayist, and poet in Toronto. He is the author of the poetry collections *Bloom* and *The Scarborough,* and the non-fiction books *Strike Anywhere* and *The Human Scale.* A contributing editor at *Toronto Life* and *Maclean's,* he is the Co-Executive Producer of a forthcoming Apple TV+ series adapted from his story "The Sting."

A note on the type

This book is typeset in Dante MT Pro, an updated version of Dante, which Giovanni Mardersteig began designing for Officina Bodini when printing resumed after World War II. This digital version was re-drawn by Monotype's Ron Carpenter. Titles are set in HEX Projects's Margo Condensed, a contemporary typeface inspired by the hand-lettering popular on mid-century book jackets and movie posters.

Printed by Imprimerie Gauvin
Gatineau, Québec